The Power of the Hawkstone

The Spirals Series

Plays

Jan Carew
Computer Killer

Chris Culshaw
Dribs and Drabs
Gaffs and Laughs
Radio Riff-Raff

Christine Dawe
The Wanna Beez

Julia Donaldson
Books and Crooks

Nigel Gray
An Earwig in the Ear

Angela Griffiths
TV Hospital
Wally and Co

Paul Groves
Tell Me Where it Hurts

Julia Pattison
Kicking Up a Stink

Bill Ridgway
Monkey Business

John Townsend
A Bit of a Shambles
Cheer and Groan
Chef's Night Off
Clogging the Works
Cowboys, Jelly and Custard
Gulp and Gasp
Hiccups and Slip-ups
Jumping the Gun
A Lot of Old Codswallop
A Maggot in the Mouthwash
Murder at Muckleby Manor

David Walke
The Good, the Bad and the Bungle
Package Holiday

Non-fiction

Jim Alderson
Crash in the Jungle

Jan Carew
Eyam, Plague Village

Chris Culshaw
Dive into Danger
Ground Zero

David Orme
Hackers

Jill Ridge
Lifelines

Bill Ridgway
Break Out!
Lost in Alaska
Over the Wall
A Soldiers Tale

Julie Taylor
Lucky Dip

John Townsend
Burke and Hare: The Body Snatchers
Kingdom of the Man-eaters
Raiders of the Dome Diamond
Trapped Under Ground

Keith West
Back to the Wild
The Great Trek

Fiction

Jim Alderson
The Witch Princess

Penny Bates
Tiger of the Lake

Jan Carew
Footprints in the Sand
Voices in the Dark

Susan Duberley
The Ring

John Goodwin
Ghost Train

Angela Griffiths
Diary of a Wild Thing
Stories of Suspense

Anita Jackson
The Actor
The Austin Seven
Bennet Manor
Dreams
The Ear
A Game of Life and Death
No Rent to Pay

Paul Jennings
Eye of Evil
Maggot

Richard Kemble
Grandmother's Secret

Helen Lowerson
The Biz

Margaret Loxton
The Dark Shadow

Bill Ridgway
The Hawkstone
The Last Trip to Oron
The Power of the Hawkstone
Mr Punch
Spots

John Townsend
Back on the Prowl
Beware the Morris Minor
A Minute to Kill
Night Beast
Snow Beast
Sweet Dreams

NEW Spirals

FICTION

The Power of the Hawkstone

Bill Ridgway

Published in 2004 by:
Nelson Thornes Ltd
Delta Place
27 Bath Road
CHELTENHAM
GL53 7TH
United Kingdom

04 05 06 07 08 / 10 9 8 7 6 5 4 3 2 1

A catalogue record for this book is available from the British Library

ISBN 0 7487 9002 0

Cover illustration by Janek Matysiak
Page make-up by Tech-Set, Gateshead

Printed in Croatia by Zrinski

1

It was autumn, and the first chill winds blew across the plains. My father sat by the log fire. He hardly spoke. When he did speak, it was of Morpeth.

Morpeth had wanted to rule the plains. He had almost killed my father. Now Morpeth was dead. His body had turned to bones. I'd watched them fall one by one into the Pit of Fire.

My father had been a brave man. In his youth no one could match him. I hoped I would be as brave. And as wise. The people of the plains had much to thank him for. They were free from Morpeth's grasp for ever.

For some days I had felt ill at ease. Something troubled me. I did not know what. Now I found myself at the window. Night was falling. Far away the Hawkstone rose into the dark sky. A point of light shone from Albin's cottage high on the Hawkstone. Albin was the magician who lived there.

As I looked at the speck of light it seemed to grow bigger. Now it was like a bright star. A face grew within the star. It was the face of Albin. The room got dark. Now Albin's pale face flickered like a flame before me.

'Philip . . . come to the Hawkstone . . . come tonight . . . do not delay.'

The face faded. I found myself gazing at the point of light. It vanished as I watched.

I turned back into the room. My father was sleeping. Albin had called me. Something was wrong. I must go to him. I told the servant to get my horse ready. I asked him to tell my father I had gone to Albin on the Hawkstone.

When I left the city, night had come. The plains were white in the moonlight. I took the road through the wood. Soon the trees hid the mass of rock they called the Hawkstone.

The only sounds were the horse's hooves on the stones and the dry leaves in the wind.

2

The road ran like a snake through the wood. Bars of moonlight fell between the trees. Black leaves blew in the air.

I kept a hand on my sword. I did not know what might be hiding in the darkness. I felt eyes upon me. I had taken that path many times before, and always with a feeling of danger.

As I came out of the wood the Hawkstone rose before me. The tower at its peak stood black against the moon. Its rock walls shone a deep blue.

I crossed the stream which ran at its base. I parted the bushes which hid the passage into the Hawkstone. A single torch lit the way upwards. My sword glowed in the weak light.

I came to a rope bridge. It spanned a deep gap in the rock. My horse would go no further. I tied it to a tree and set off on foot. Albin's home was not far.

As I drew near his cottage his white monkey, Tag, suddenly jumped in front of me. It knew me from my visits before. It ran ahead, leading the way. Now the yellow light from Albin's window made a bar across the path.

I was about to knock when the door opened. Albin stood there. He was a huge man, as strong as an ox. 'Philip. I have been expecting you.'

We went inside. He pointed to the table and set a glass before me. 'You need my help?' I asked.

'Yes.'

'It is not often a magician seeks my help.'

Albin went over to the window. He looked out into the shadows. 'My daughter has gone,' he said. 'Belinda has been taken.'

'Gone? What do you mean?'

He came over to the table and sat down. His deep eyes looked into mine. 'She had gone into the town. Someone is sick there. I gave her herbs to take. Perhaps I should have taken more care. Since Morpeth died, I thought there would be no more danger. I was wrong, Philip.'

'But who has taken her?'

'I believe someone has taken Morpeth's place, Philip. I do not know who it is. But I think I know their plan. Like Morpeth, they want to rule the cities of the plains. Morpeth tried and failed. But it now seems Morpeth was not alone.'

'Why do you say that?' I asked.

'The cities cannot fall while I have power. Magic can be used for good or ill. I have always tried to use it for good. But it is the Hawkstone that makes my power strong. If I were to leave the Hawkstone, I would lose my strength. I would be as weak as any other man. It is then the cities would fall.'

'But you have not left the Hawkstone,' I said.

'That is why Belinda has been taken. Someone wants me to leave the Hawkstone to look for her. If I leave I will be in danger. I will be killed. That is why I want you to bring her back, Philip. That is why I need your help.' He saw the look in my eyes and added, 'Do not worry, Philip. I will help you.'

He had left his chair. Now he began to walk up and down in the dim light. I had never seen Albin worried. He had always been strong. Now I saw another side to him. His magic did not stop him feeling what any father would feel for his child.

'You say someone has taken Belinda,' I said. 'But she may have hurt herself. Even now she might be lying by the road. Anything could have happened.'

'Trust me, Philip,' Albin said. 'I will show you.'

I watched as he took a silver ring from his robe.

3

In the ring was a dark stone. It glowed in the dim light. Albin held up the ring before my eyes. 'Look into the stone, Philip,' he said.

I wondered what he could mean.

'Look into the stone,' he said again, softly. 'Put all other thoughts from your mind. Look into the stone . . .'

I drew close to it. I tried to shut out Albin and the room. I stared into the dark stone for a long time. The room dimmed, and the stone seemed to fill it.

The dark colour faded. I could see shadows forming. Dark clouds. I stared deeper into the stone. It seemed to draw me in. The shadows got sharper. Now they were turning into a picture.

I saw Belinda. She was in a cave. There were torches on the walls. Behind her the rock looked like a strange dragon. The cave glowed in the torch light.

Belinda was sitting on a ledge. She had a cloth around her shoulders, as if she was trying to keep out the cold. By her side was a jug and bowl. There was no one else in the cave.

As I gazed into the ring, Belinda turned. She seemed to be looking right at me. She opened her mouth to say something. But at that moment she turned once more into shadow. The cave melted into darkness.

I rubbed my eyes. Albin put the ring back in his robe. 'She is being held in the Dragon Cave,' he said. 'I do not know who has taken her there. Whoever it is will be waiting for me to leave the Hawkstone to look for her. They might even be waiting below as we speak. They dare not come up here. Yet it would not help Belinda if I were to leave.'

'Does she know I have seen her in the ring?' I asked.

'She knows,' he said. 'We each have a ring. The stones are very powerful. They may be used in times of danger.'

'And do your enemies know of these rings?'

Albin was silent for a time. 'I do not think so,' he said at last. 'Belinda still has her ring. Had they known its power they would have taken it from her. But it would have done them no good. Few can use the ring. Its power is mine to use as I wish.'

Tag had come into the room. He jumped onto Albin's shoulder. 'There is little time to spare,' Albin said. 'Will you bring Belinda back, Philip?'

Albin had helped me in the past. He had saved my father, too. I would bring Belinda back to the Hawkstone. Not only to repay Albin. Belinda had been a friend. Now, she was more than a friend. I would do anything to free her from danger.

4

Albin told me to leave the Hawkstone by night. The cave was on an island a short way across the sea. The Hawkstone looked out over the sea on one side. From the tower, Dragon Island was a black hump with moonlit water all around it.

'My enemies will soon be waiting for me to leave the Hawkstone,' Albin said. 'They will come at first light. I am sure of it. They must not know you have been here, Philip. I will show you a hidden path.'

I followed Albin up to the tower. As we walked, he told me where a boat was hidden. 'There is something else, too,' he said as we reached the tower door.

'What is that?'

'Dragon Cave was used by Morpeth. He used to shut his enemies there until they died of hunger or madness. To make sure they did not escape he had them guarded. I fear the guard is still there. For Belinda.'

'Do you know who he is?' I asked. 'Is he a warrior?'

Albin shook his head. 'His name is Gorex. This guard is like no other, for he can take many forms.'

I asked him what he meant.

'He can be an eagle or a snake. A lion or a vulture. Few can escape while such a being guards the cave.'

'Then I fear we may never see Belinda again,' I said. 'I am not afraid of death. Yet I can be no match for such powers.'

Albin smiled. 'You will not have to face Gorex without my help, Philip. As long as I stay on the Hawkstone, my powers are as great as his. Greater, perhaps. We shall see.'

He opened the door of the tower and went in. I wondered why he had brought me to that place. He put his hand against a large stone set in the wall. There was a noise, like the grinding of a mill. As I watched, the unicorn at the base of the tower moved to one side. Steps led down into the darkness.

'These will take you to the sea,' he said. 'You will find the boat on the beach. Good luck, Philip. And do not worry. I will not let you fight alone. Here. Take this.'

He took from his belt a small bag. He handed it to me. I asked him what was in it.

‘I told you Gorex could take many forms,’ Albin said. ‘I did not tell you he can also be invisible. There is magic dust in the bag. When you get near the cave, open the bag and tip the dust out. I will do the rest.’

I did not know what to make of this. But I trusted Albin. I took the first step into the darkness. When I turned to thank him he was nowhere to be seen.

I wondered if he had been there at all. Albin was full of surprises.

5

I found the boat and pushed it into the water. I wanted to reach the island before the sky grew light. Two oars lay in the bottom of the boat. I began to row out to sea. A light wind rippled the water as I struck out.

As I drew near the island, I could make out tall cliffs. There was a line of foam where the waves beat upon the stones. The first blush of dawn lit the morning sky. I rowed harder. I wanted to get to land before day came.

A faint mist hung over the sea. I faced the Hawkstone as I rowed. Now it grew small, a faint finger of rock pointing into the sky. A moment later I entered a small bay. A pebble beach ran upwards.

It was very still. Any sound might send a signal to Belinda's guard. Or to others who had brought her there. I pulled the boat out of the water. I turned it over and hid it in clumps of seaweed.

I wondered what to do. I might already have been seen. An invisible being would have invisible eyes. Even now it might be watching me.

But if it was watching me, it would attack me. And so far I was safe. I felt that somehow Albin would protect me. I knew I could trust him.

I crept upwards. From the top of the rocks I looked out over the sea. The mist had gone, and the sun was brighter. It was then I saw a speck far off on the water. It was a boat. And it was sailing towards the Hawkstone. I remembered what Albin had said. 'They will expect me to leave the Hawkstone at first light. Then I will be as weak as any other man. They will attack me. They might even kill me . . .'

Who was in the boat? Were they fishermen from the Plains? Or were they the visitors Albin expected? I could not tell. There was nothing I could do. I had one task. To bring Belinda back to the Hawkstone.

I felt the bag of dust at my side. With my hand on my sword, I crept away from the beach.

The land was covered with wild grass and wind-bent trees. I did not know which way to go. I could see no path. There was nothing to tell me where Belina was.

A voice in my head whispered to Albin. I felt a sudden gust of wind. I drew my sword. A little way ahead was a tall rock. It looked like an evil face. My mouth went dry. Albin had said Gorex could take many forms. Was I looking at Gorex now?

I fixed my eyes on the rock. I kept my sword ready. But instead of Gorex, the rock changed to the face of Albin.

'Philip . . . Philip . . . '

His voice was like the sigh of the wind.

'Where shall I go?' I asked.

'Gorex has many eyes and ears. You must take great care. Come closer to the stone.'

I walked slowly forward. Albin seemed to look down on me from above. 'Walk to the hill where a single tree grows. From the hill you will see the cave. Go to the hill but no further. I will show you what to do.'

His face melted into the rock. I looked around. I saw the hill and went towards it. I stood in the shadow of the tree. There was no sound. The air was still. Far off I could see a deep gash in the cliff. A faint light came from within.

I crept behind the tree and lay against its trunk. A sudden tiredness came over me. As my eyes closed, I saw Albin. I must have slept for most of the day. When I awoke, the sun was fading and a bright moon had risen over the sea.

6

I rubbed my eyes and looked toward the cave. The faint light still shone through the gloom. A cool night air crept over the island. I pulled my cloak around me. I felt hungry and alone. Yet Albin had not yet told me what I must do.

I sat with my back to the tree waiting for darkness to come. Did Belinda know I was on the island? Perhaps her father had given her a signal. They each had a ring. It would not be hard for him to show her what was happening.

'Are you ready, Philip?'

Albin's voice jolted me out of my thoughts. It seemed to come from inside the tree. I turned my head.

'Take the bag from your belt. Pour the dust into your hand.'

I did as he asked. The dust sparkled as it fell. I closed my hand on it. A faint tingle ran through my fingers. I had heard people speak of stardust. I wondered if this was the same.

'Walk to the cave . . . When the wind blows, open your fingers and let the dust fly . . . Remember, Philip . . . let the dust fly.'

I began to walk towards the cave. I was getting near the end of my journey. A cold fear made my heart beat like a drum. Soon I would be face to face with an invisible enemy. How could I fight something I could not see?

The moon made shadows across the land. I crept through them towards the cave. As I drew near, a gust of wind rippled my cloak. A cloud was forming in the dark sky. As I watched, it turned to the form of Albin. His body was drawn out like smoke, his beard trailing across the moon.

He blew the wind that tugged at my cloak. Over the noise I heard his voice. 'Let the dust fly, Philip . . . let the dust fly . . .'

I opened my hand. The dust rose into the air like a swarm of silver butterflies. Then something odd happened. Something which filled me with fear. The dust hit the invisible Gorex. It clung to every part of him. The outline of a huge monster rose up. It had the face and body of a man, but a goat's legs. Sparks shot from its body and hit my sword. The sword flashed as the sparks hit it.

Gorex turned his red eyes to me. He let out a wild scream and took a step towards me.

7

Gorex towered above me. One blow would kill me. What use would my sword be against such a monster? I looked at the giant head. His teeth flashed in the moonlight like flint knives. Fear crept into my heart.

Then into my mind came Belinda. For a moment I thought I saw her in the cave. I remembered Albin's worried face. I knew he would not let harm come to me. I knew he must still be there at my side.

My grip on the sword grew strong. I felt a new power creep into my arms. Gorex gave a roar which bent the grass. I looked up into his fire-red eyes.

Suddenly, he changed. No longer did he have the shape of a man. Now he was a giant bird. Its wings spread wide before me. Its huge beak was a spear, ready to strike.

I felt the power grow in my sword arm. Without my will, my sword began to swing. Faster and faster it flew. Some force was making it move. It must be Albin.

The great bird rose high in the air. For a moment it was lost in the night sky. Then, with a rush, it swooped down to scoop me up. The power now surged in my legs. As the huge beak was about to strike, I jumped clear.

The bird hit the rocks. It lay for a moment, stunned. It was then I saw my chance. A step took me to the bird's twisting neck. I lifted my sword. With all my strength I brought it down.

A fountain of black blood sprayed upwards. My sword had cut clean through the bird's neck. Now its head and body lay apart. I felt the power leave me. I sat on a stone and put my head in my hands. For a time I forgot what I'd come to the cave to do.

When I looked up I felt a jolt of fear. The thing before me was moving. The neck and head were creeping towards the body. Then something stranger happened. The bird became two halves of a snake. The halves moved towards each other. I knew if they joined, the fight would start all over again. This time I might not win – even with Albin's help.

Then I remembered the torch just inside the cave. In a moment I had the torch in my hand and brought it to the head of the twisting snake. The fire bit into its scaly body. There was a gush of flame. The head jerked from side to side. As it burnt it changed once more into a bird. Then to a man's head again.

It roared with rage as it flamed. Then it fell to the ground. The flames died. The monster was no more than a black patch in the grass. Then that, too, vanished.

I stood in silence outside the cave. Then, holding the torch high, I went in.

8

I kept my sword ready as I walked further into the cave. Water plopped from the roof and echoed in the darkness. I saw bats clinging to the walls. In another place a spike of rock jabbed upwards.

I called Belinda's name. The sound echoed from the walls. I waited. Then I heard a faint cry. I hurried on. The cave grew wider. I found myself in a huge cavern.

It was some time before I got used to the dim light. Then I saw Belinda. She was sitting on a stone, tied to a rocky spike. Quickly I cut the rope which held her.

'Philip,' she said. 'Where is Gorex?'

'Gorex is dead.'

'But . . .'

'I think we should go,' I said. 'I still feel danger here. Your father will be waiting. We must leave the island before it gets light.'

She rose to her feet. She seemed weak, and I put my arm around her. She took a step forward and stopped.

'What is it?' I asked.

She pulled something from her shoe. It was the ring. 'I hid it,' she said. 'I didn't want them to see what my father was doing.'

'Them? Who do you mean?' I asked.

'Let us leave this place. I will tell you.'

The grass was dark under our feet. We ran past the tree towards the sea. The moon made a silver path across the water. Quickly I pushed out the boat and took the oars. I must reach the Hawkstone before the sun came up. Gorex was gone. But Belinda had hinted at other dangers.

Far out, the Hawkstone rose from the water. 'Who were you talking about in the cave?' I said.

'Do you remember Morpeth?' she asked.

'I remember him. He died in the Pit of Fire.'

'Morpeth had helpers,' she said.

'The Keeper was his spy,' I said. 'But he is dead. He fell from the tower. What other helpers did Morpeth have?'

'Do you remember Morpeth was fool enough to come to the Hawkstone? He had a small band of men with him. He was going to kill your father. Do you remember, Philip?'

'You cut the rope bridge,' I said. 'Only Morpeth got across. The others died in the fall.'

Belinda smiled grimly. 'I thought so too. I was wrong. One of Morpeth's men did not die. He fell onto a ledge. I have found out his name. Elidor. He vows to carry on Morpeth's work. He will not rest until the cities of the plains are in his grasp.'

'How do you know this?' I asked.

'Caves echo,' she said. 'I heard Elidor and his men plotting. They wanted my father to come for me. My father is the only one who can stop their new army. You came instead, Philip.'

'We must return to the Hawkstone without delay,' I said. 'Elidor will be waiting at dawn for Albin to search for you. By now he will know your father has sent someone else to bring you back. If your father thinks I have failed, he will leave the Hawkstone to look for you himself.'

The oars skimmed over the water. The sky was turning grey. 'Elidor will not be pleased when he finds I am gone,' Belinda said. 'I am his bait.'

'Then we must row harder,' I said. 'We shall soon be safe.'

It was then I noticed a boat. It was still far off. But it was coming towards us. Belinda saw where I was looking. She let out a gasp. 'Elidor,' she said.

9

The boat was getting close. Belinda looked into the ring her father had given to her. Her mind was locked into the stone. At last she looked up. She pointed ahead to the Hawkstone. 'Look, Philip. My father is standing on the tower. Do not worry. He has seen us in his ring. He will not let harm come to us.'

Elidor's boat was closer now. Its sail hissed in the wind. I could see three men in the boat. I drew my sword and laid it across the seat. They must have seen us from far off. Maybe Elidor had kept a watch for anyone leaving the island.

The boat was almost on us. One of the men stood. He held a hook fixed to a rope. When he came up to us, he would throw the hook over our boat to bring both boats together. I let the oars drop and picked up my sword.

Then came a roll of thunder. I looked towards Albin on the tower. As I watched, a dart of fire flew down. It struck Elidor's boat. Flames flickered from its sail. One of the men cut the sail down. It fell across the boat, and the three of them tried to push it into the sea.

In their haste they forgot us. We took up our oars and pulled. We were now in the shadow of the Hawkstone.

Elidor's boat fell back. I saw the burning sail sink into the sea. We were not far from the shore. 'I told you my father would help us,' said Belinda.

I smiled. Then my smile froze. Elidor was following us again. Now they were rowing. We rowed harder. But the gap between us was closing. Below our boat the rocks made shadows in the water. We were under the Hawkstone. We could no longer see Albin. But we knew he must still be up the tower. For at that moment another dart sped through the air. It hit the water to the side of Elidor's boat.

A jet of water flew upwards. The sea around Elidor's boat began to boil. It spun like a whirlpool. His boat spun with it. A hole opened in the sea. Elidor's boat spun towards the hole. I heard the men cry out. They were past help. As I watched, their boat was sucked down into the darkness.

The sea became calm again. We stopped rowing. Nothing came to the surface. No boat. No part of the boat. No Elidor. We pulled at the oars again. A moment later the boat was scraping the pebbles.

10

Albin was standing on the beach as I brought the boat in. Belinda climbed out. Her father held her for a moment.

We made our way up the Hawkstone. I felt tired and hungry. Belinda sat quietly at the table. After we had eaten, Albin said we should rest.

I awoke in the afternoon. Tag sat on the bed, eating a nut. He followed me into the next room. Belinda was already up. She was talking to her father.

'I hope you feel better for your rest,' he said when he saw me.

'Yes,' I said. 'Belinda seems well, too.'

'In future she must take care,' Albin said. 'And so must I. When she leaves the Hawkstone again, she will be safe.'

'Can you be sure, father?' Belinda asked.

'Elidor has followed Morpeth to his doom,' Albin said. 'The plains will be safe now. And so will you.'

I looked at Albin. He was smiling. He was wise. And powerful. I hoped he was right. The next day I set off for home under a cool sun. Belinda stood with Albin to wave me off.

I had promised to see her again before long. My journey home would give me time to ponder over the last few days. And to wonder what else fate had in store.

If you enjoyed this story, why not try the first NEW SPIRALS story:

The Hawkstone by Bill Ridgway